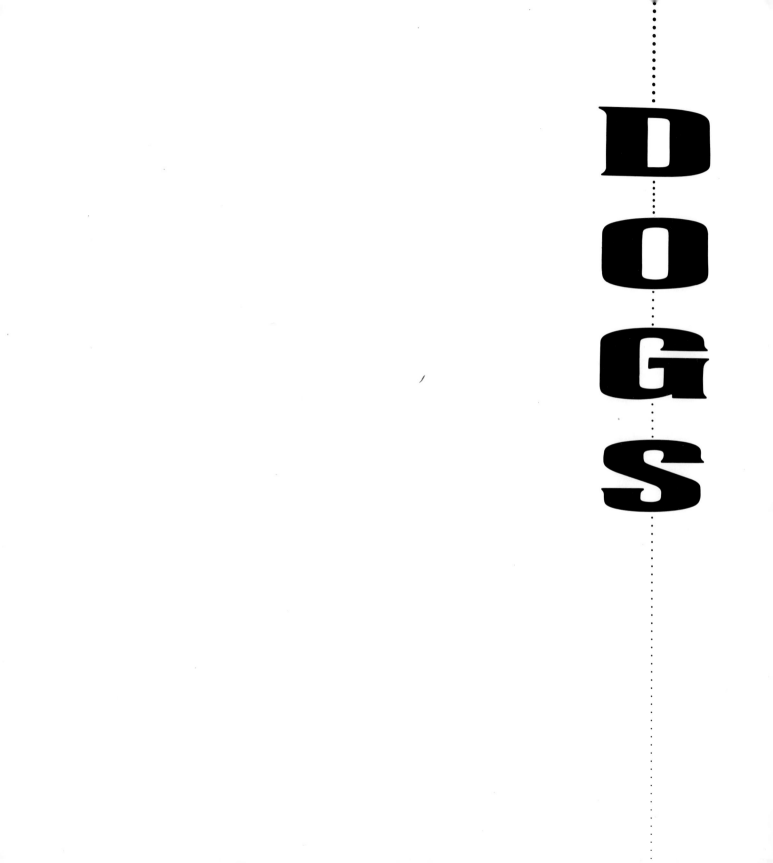

DOGS

DOGS

The Wolf
Within

*By
Dorothy
Hinshaw
Patent*

*photographs
by
William
Muñoz*

Carolrhoda Books, Inc.
Minneapolis

To the memory of Chester and Lena,
two of the best friends anyone could have.

The author and photographer wish to thank the following people for their help with this book: Grover, Laura, and Erin Barr; Jane Callaway; Diane Carrell; the Cox family; Suzie Foley; Ken and Barbara Jolley; Glenn Martyn; Sean Muñoz; Jerry Noble; Jason Patent; Amy and Corey Peters; Barbara Smith; Roland Smith; Lindsay Smith; with special thanks to Neil and Karin. And thanks to all their canine companions. Thanks also to the Lee Metcalf National Wildlife Refuge, the Missoula County Humane Society, Rio Grande Zoo in Albuquerque, and Wolf Scat Ranch.

The publisher would like to thank L. David Mech, wolf biologist, and Dr. Joseph Quigley and Ruth Foster, Center to Study Human-Animal Relationships and Environments, University of Minnesota, for their assistance with this book.

Ruth Berman, Series Editor
Zachary Marell, Series Designer

Photograph on page 8 courtesy of Paula Jansen © 1990

Words that appear in **bold** type are listed in the glossary on page 47.

Library of Congress Cataloging-in-Publication Data

Patent, Dorothy Hinshaw.
  Dogs : the wolf within / by Dorothy Hinshaw Patent ; photographs by William Muñoz.
      p.   cm. — (Understanding animals)
  Includes index.
  Summary: Compares the physical characteristics and behavior of wolves and dogs and describes how dogs evolved from their wild relatives.
    ISBN 0-87614-691-4 (lib. bdg.)
    ISBN 0-87614-604-3 (pbk.)
    1. Dogs—Behavior—Juvenile literature. 2. Wolves—Behavior-Juvenile literature. [1. Dogs—Habits and behavior. 2. Wolves-Habits and behavior.] I. Title. II. Series.
SF433.P37 1993
599.74'442—dc20   92-12334
                                                                CIP
                                                                AC

Manufactured in the United States of America

1   2   3   4   5   6   98   97   96   95   94   93

This book is available in two editions:
Library binding by Carolrhoda Books, Inc.,
Soft cover by First Avenue Editions
241 First Avenue North
Minneapolis, Minnesota 55401

Contents

Chapter 1

Where Dogs Come From

Wolf pups are appealing to humans.

No one knows how it happened, how humans more than 12,000 years ago got the idea to tame the wolf. Early humans certainly knew this great animal hunter, and they must have admired its strength, speed, and intelligence. Wolves, in turn, may have hung around the edges of human settlements, snatching discarded bones or feeding from the remains left after people took the meat from their kills. Perhaps orphaned wolf pups were adopted by people who later brought them along on hunts, taking advantage of the wolf's speed and fine sense of smell. Or maybe tame wolves were used as camp sentinels and protectors. We may not know what caused people to take up with wolves, but we do know the result—the dog, the first animal to be taken from the wild and changed over time to suit human society. In the process of developing an animal that looks to us for guidance and serves our needs, we have

Opposite: *The wolf is a beautiful animal and a great hunter.*

7

altered the wolf, eliminating some traits, retaining others, and emphasizing those we found of value.

ORIGIN OF THE DOG

As humans during prehistoric times expanded their range, they encountered the wolf, a four-legged animal that lived so much like they did. Because of their similarities, the two species came quickly to understand one another. This understanding led to one of the most successful and extensive cooperations between species on earth—the partnership between humans and their **canine** companions. The partnership was so natural that it is likely that the idea of **taming** wolves occurred over and over again, wherever humans and wolves shared the land.

This petroglyph found on the Hopi Reservation in Arizona is dated between 1200 and 1300 B.C. The rock carving shows three dogs (lower right) chasing wild animals.

Barbara and Spring communicate well with one another.

Unfortunately, as human society has moved farther away from its origins in nature, we have lost much of our ancient ability to relate to dogs as fellow social, feeling beings. By looking at the behavior of the dog's wild ancestor, the wolf, we can hope better to understand its **domesticated** descendant, the dog.

WOLVES AND HUMANS

What made the wolf such a natural partner for people? Perhaps more than any other creature, the animal scientists call *Canis lupus*, the gray wolf, has a society that mirrors that of humans. While humans were **evolving** into cooperative hunters in Africa and perhaps parts of Asia, gray wolves were fulfilling the same role all across the Northern Hemisphere.

Right: *Deer are common prey for wolves.*

Wolves bury leftovers in the ground to be dug up when food is scarce. This ancient need to protect against possible hunger is the reason some dogs destroy beautiful lawns burying toys or bones.

Both species hunted large animals. Bringing down big prey requires cooperation among members of a hunting team as well as a means of communication for the hunt. Obedience to leaders is necessary as well as the ability to learn from experience.

Once the prey was brought down, hunters shared what they had killed, both with one another and with the members of their group who hadn't participated in the hunt. To keep the society running smoothly, each individual knew his or her social position. All individuals also were willing to serve the needs of the group even if doing so might have conflicted with their own wishes.

WHY ONLY THE WOLF?

Wolves and dogs belong to the scientific family Canidae, which includes many different animals. Why was the gray wolf the only species in the entire canid family that was domesticated? Humans and wolves share the qualities of living in a social, or pack, society. The closest relatives to gray wolves in the canid family are jackals, coyotes, and red wolves (which some scientists believe are actually not a separate species). The several species of jackals, which live in Africa or Asia, are generally solitary hunters, even though they may sometimes associate in family groups. The American coyote can also form family packs, but this behavior is probably relatively infrequent, one that the animals use to bring down large prey in areas where wolves no longer live. We know little about the behavior of the red wolf, which is native to the American Southeast, since most red wolves were killed off in the early days of settling the country.

The rest of the family Canidae, such as foxes and maned wolves, are not closely related to gray wolves. The African hunting dog, a rather distant relative, is the only other canid known to hunt consistently in packs. African hunting dogs have a close social organization, and they share food with one another. Most experts do think that the wolf is the only dog ancestor. Wolves and dogs are different enough that scientists consider them separate species and call the dog *Canis familiaris.*

Coyotes sometimes hunt in packs, but more often they live alone or in pairs, except when raising young.

African hunting dogs hunt in packs, but they aren't organized the same way as wolf packs.

Dominance Hierarchy

Dominant Alpha Pair

*Subordinate Wolf
with Pups*

Below: *Male and female
wolves get along well to-
gether.*

THE WOLF PACK

The cooperative hunting group of wolves is actually a family unit called a pack. A pack usually consists of a pair of wolves and their offspring from previous years. The top male is called the alpha male, after the first letter in the Greek alphabet. The number one female is the alpha female. In a sense, these two are the leaders of the pack. They are usually the parents of the pups. They are in the prime of life and are wise and experienced.

The social order of the pack is maintained through a **dominance hierarchy.** This means that each wolf has its own rank in the pack. The alpha male and female are at the top of the hierarchy, and the youngest wolves are usually at the bottom. The other pack members are in between. The males have their own dominance hierarchy and the females have theirs. A male may challenge a higher-ranking male or a female may challenge a female, but the two genders don't normally fight with each other. The lowest-ranking wolf may be picked on by the other pack members and forced to leave the pack,

A subordinate wolf licks the muzzle of a more dominant pack mate.

becoming a lone wolf and wandering off into new territory. Such a lone wolf may find a mate and start a new pack.

Wolf packs aren't always set up in exactly this way. Sometimes a pack, especially a smaller one, will accept a lone wolf. Now and then, one of the other females besides the alpha may produce a litter of pups, and a non-alpha male may succeed in breeding. As an alpha animal grows older, a younger wolf may challenge its authority and eventually take over the alpha role.

Whatever the relationships among the adults, the whole pack helps take care of the pups. As a matter of fact, a human observer who doesn't know who the parents are would not be able to pick them out based on the animals' behavior. When the pups are very young, the mother must stay with them while the other wolves hunt. But the pack members bring food home to her, so she needn't go hungry. When the pups get older and are eating meat, the mother may go hunting while a different wolf "babysits" the pups. The returning hunters carry food in their stomachs for the pups and the babysitter. The pups lick at the mouths of the returning wolves. This licking induces the hunters to regurgitate food from their stomachs for the pups to eat.

Wolf pups are cared for by the whole pack, not just their mother.

The lower wolf is behaving in a submissive way. Note the pricked ears of the dominant wolf compared to the flat ears of the subordinate.

The dominant wolf on top has pricked ears and a tail raised up high. The subordinate wolf's tail is tucked under in a sign of submission.

SOCIAL RELATIONSHIPS

The relationships among wolves in a pack show in their behavior. Starting when they are young, the pups are part of the dominance hierarchy. The pups are **subordinate,** or low in the dominance hierarchy, and act **submissively**, while the other wolves in the pack behave in a dominant fashion toward the pups. A dominant animal approaches a subordinate with its ears pricked forward, its tail held high, and sometimes with its hackles, or the fur on its shoulders, raised. The subordinate responds by folding its ears back, holding its tail down, and crouching. If the dominant animal comes right up to it, the subordinate is likely to roll over on its back, perhaps pawing gently at the dominant one. Often, the submissive wolf urinates while on its back.

As the pups grow older, they romp and play together. In their play, they practice the roles of dominant and subordinate wolf. One pup stands over its littermate, who lies submissively on the ground. But in a few minutes, the roles may

be reversed. The pups also do a lot of play fighting, which strengthens their muscles and teaches them the skills they will later need in bringing down prey.

Dominant wolves generally get what they want. After a successful hunt, the alpha pair feeds before the other pack members. The alpha male can usually keep the younger males from breeding, and the alpha female normally does the same with the others of her gender. Often, all that it takes to make a subordinate cringe away is an intense, direct stare.

Even though order is maintained through the dominance hierarchy, the pack members are very affectionate with one another. When an animal returns after a solitary hunt, the other animals crowd around, wagging their tails and greeting it enthusiastically. After sleeping and before a hunt, all the pack members may join together in excited playful behavior that climaxes in a group howl.

Young pups practice displaying submissive and dominant behaviors.

A subordinate wolf (right) reacts to a dominant wolf's stare (left) by backing away and allowing the dominant wolf to eat undisturbed.

Chapter 2

Domestication
of the Dog

Elsa would rather be indoors with people than be alone outside.

*I*t's hard to believe that all dogs are one and the same species. Dogs come in so many sizes, shapes, and colors. Their ears, tails, coats, and heads vary so much it seems strange they all began long ago as wolves. But through the process of domestication, big changes in wild species can come about.

Taming is the first step in domestication. But there is a big difference between taming and domestication. An individual wild animal, especially one raised by humans, may become tame and not fear people. But domestication is another matter. The process of domestication involves **selective breeding** of animals over many generations, altering the physical appearance and modifying the psychological makeup of a species in order to make the animals useful to people and compatible with human society.

Opposite: *It's hard to believe that a smooth-haired, 110-pound rottweiler, and a wavy-haired, 3-pound teacup poodle are the same species.*

17

Dogs must be able to include people as part of their pack and allow us to fulfill their social needs. Here, dog and child are clearly enjoying their friendship.

Wolves depend only on fellow pack members to fulfill their social needs.

CHANGES IN BEHAVIOR

Many things happen to a species when it is domesticated. The most important changes are those in behavior.

Wild animals respond to new situations with fear and caution. But a domesticated animal has become adaptable. It must be able to accept new environments without becoming too frightened. Social wild animals like wolves look to one another for attention and protection. But when domesticated species like dogs live away from others of their own kind, they look to humans to meet their social needs. At the same time, domesticated species must be able to accept humans as leaders, so that people can control them.

How can such big changes in temperament come about? The personalities of individuals are as different in other species as they are in our own. In a litter of wolf pups, some may be fearful while others are adventuresome. Some might form

Individuals within a species have different personalities. The wolf on the right is more cautious and fearful than the wolf on the left.

Wolves that were especially friendly to people were probably chosen as human companions and helpers, becoming the ancestors to today's domestic dogs.

closer relationships with humans than others. And, to varying degrees, some are more likely to accept dominant behavior from people and follow the lead of humans. The individuals with the most desirable behaviors would be the ones most likely to be kept and bred. Since an animal's basic temperament is partially inherited, humans shape the behavior of their companions, even if they don't do so consciously.

NATURAL VARIATIONS

How did the physical differences among dogs come about? Nature provides many kinds of physical variations as well as temperamental ones that humans can choose from when they domesticate an animal. The shape and proportions of the body of individuals of a species differ—for example, some have longer legs than others, or bigger ears. Unusual colors can show up, too.

Through selective breeding, black wolves (above) and multi-colored gray wolves (right) helped produce the color variations we see in domestic dogs.

In nature, individuals with especially abnormal body proportions or colors that make them stand out might not survive. For example, short legs can mean slow running, and an unusual color can make an animal easy for prey or for enemies to spot. But such differences attract humans, who breed the unusual animals and preserve their traits. Over thousands of years, just such selection has resulted in the hundreds of breeds of dogs living in the world today.

Wolves offered plenty of natural variation for people to select from. Among large mammals, the wolf's geographical range was second only to that of humans, and in different areas, wolves developed quite a variety of traits. The differences in size are the most obvious. A male Arabian wolf weighs around 35 to 45 pounds, while a male Alaskan tundra wolf can be more than three times heavier. The normal colors can be quite variable, also. Wolves today can be many shades of brown and gray as well as white and black. The longer guard hairs that overlie the soft undercoat of a "gray" wolf can actually consist of bands of five colors—black, brown, gray, red, and white. And every now and then, an unusual color or combination of colors turns up.

SELECTIVE BREEDING

Once people realized that they could influence the appearance and temperament of their dogs through careful choosing of mates, they were on their way toward the development of different breeds. Probably one of the most important first steps was to produce animals that could be used to help people and could be clearly distinguished from wolves. That way, people could easily identify dogs, even from a distance. This principle probably led quite early to the typical dog tail, which curves at least slightly upward rather than being straight like a wolf's tail. In order to be able to recognize their dogs, people

Even at rest, a dog's tail curves upward.

may have also preferred the unusual colors and floppy, un-wolflike ears that we see in many breeds today.

As early as 10,000 B.C., four different subtypes of dogs seem to have existed. In northern areas lived animals similar to present-day huskies, while dogs much like modern sheepdogs lived in the Middle East and Europe. Medium-sized dogs were found throughout Europe, and a small house-dog type also existed. Egyptian murals from 1900 B.C. show a variety of dog breeds that served different functions almost four thousand years ago.

Over the thousands of years they have shared their lives with humans, dogs have become one of our most useful animal helpers. In developing different dog breeds, people have encouraged or discouraged different aspects of natural wolf behavior, depending on the job the animal is expected to perform.

Spitzlike dogs such as these Siberian huskies are an ancient type of dog. Today, huskies are used in sled racing.

Even though it has been raining hard, this Alaskan wolf can smell the scent left by a grizzly bear that had passed by an hour earlier.

The borzoi, or Russian wolfhound, is a sight hound. Ironically, borzois were developed to hunt their own ancestor, the wolf.

SIGHT VERSUS SCENT

Wolves use their senses of sight and smell to locate prey. A group of dogs that hunts using eyesight, called sight hounds, was originally bred in the deserts of northern Africa to help people hunt swift animals such as gazelles. In addition to selecting for superior vision, sight hound breeders worked on developing the fastest dogs possible, dogs that would chase anything that ran. The result was not only a swift hunter but also a perfect racer—American greyhounds, for example, are racing dogs, providing entertainment for thousands of spectators in many states today.

The famous canine nose, on the other hand, has reached its finest stage of refinement in bloodhounds, a breed that can tell identical twins apart by their smell. But while bloodhounds have an incredible sense of smell, their eyesight leaves something to be desired, and their plodding gait is far from the graceful, swift sprint of the greyhound.

SPORTING DOGS

Sporting breeds have been bred for their superior sense of smell, although each may use its nose in a different way. Pointers, for example, hunt nose in the air, catching the scent of birds hidden in the brush upwind. Labrador retrievers, on the other hand, are foot trackers like bloodhounds. They keep their noses down, following tracks left by birds walking along the ground.

Once a hunting dog such as a German shorthaired pointer has located its quarry, it freezes in its tracks, indicating to a person that birds are just ahead. The hunter can then get ready to flush the bird and shoot. If the shot is successful, the dog retrieves the fallen game, gently carrying it back to the hunter in its mouth. It takes training to get a bird dog to perform reliably, but the appropriate **instincts** are already

Above: *Wolves often kill their prey far from the rest of their pack, so they have to carry food back to other pack members. This retrieving instinct has been highly encouraged in breeds like the golden retriever.*

Right: *Pointers like Greta hunt with their noses in the air.*

there. Today, some sporting dog breeds exist as two separate strains—one bred for the instincts necessary in the field and the other for the physical appearance that wins ribbons in the show ring.

The retrieving instinct probably developed from wolves' habit of bringing food back to the den for the mother and pups. It has been emphasized so strongly in retriever breeds that anyone foolish enough to throw a stick once for a retriever is usually stuck with continuing the game until his or her arm feels ready to fall off.

Above: *Labrador retrievers like Max seem to enjoy retrieving.*

Left: *Border collies concentrate intently as they work.*

HERDING AND PROTECTING

Wolves are predators and naturally run after prey animals. But they are also protective of their territory and the members of their own pack. These two traits can be bred separately and are the origins of two different types of sheepdog.

Sheepdogs like Border collies have been bred for centuries to assist shepherds. People have selected the wolf's natural

Dogs that were bred to guard sheep, like this Great Pyrenees, look somewhat like sheep and blend in with the flock.

tendency to chase after prey, along with a strong sense of the dominance hierarchy, which makes herding dogs like Border collies trainable by a strong human leader. Herding breeds are especially sensitive to approval and disapproval from people. A herding dog may chase sheep or even nip at them, but the dog can be taught to obey both voice commands and arm signals. In this way, herding dogs can get sheep to move just where the shepherd wants.

Another type of sheepdog shows very different behavior toward sheep—it guards sheep rather than chases them. Guard breed puppies are usually raised with sheep instead of with people or other dogs. They look to sheep for companionship.

When these guard dogs grow up, they behave protectively toward sheep, chasing away other dogs, coyotes, wolves, or bears that might be a threat. Unlike herding breeds, guard dogs are independently minded. Their job is not to look to people for guidance. They are on their own in the pasture, watching out for the welfare of their "pack"—the sheep. Some guard dogs are so protective that they must be tied up when it's time to round up the sheep. Otherwise they may get in the way, trying to protect the sheep from the shepherd and the herding dogs.

FIGHTING AND KILLING

Wild wolves within a pack rarely fight with one another. Their social signals are so well developed that they can reach an understanding about rank in the pack without hurting each other. Such restraint is necessary when the survival of the group depends on each individual being physically fit and able to do its part in the hunt.

Wolves have a well-developed system of social signals to prevent serious fights within the pack.

Right: *Irish terriers are energetic dogs.*

Above: *Terriers were bred not only to chase but also to follow their prey into burrows and kill them.*

But wolves do know how to fight when necessary, and they do know how to kill prey. These traits have been emphasized in a variety of ways in developing some dog breeds. Terriers, for example, were originally developed as hunters of small animals like foxes and rats that humans looked upon as pests. Whereas sporting dog breeds have the job of finding prey, like game birds, and then stopping, terriers have been bred to be fearless killers, following the prey right into underground burrows if necessary.

The traits of fearlessness and willingness to fight have, unfortunately, been exploited by people. Groups of dogs that came to be known as bulldogs, used to be set loose in a pen with a bull. People would watch while the dogs locked their jaws onto the bull's legs, head, and neck, and were tossed about by the victim's struggles to get free. Other breeds were developed to fight other dogs in a pit and came to be called pit bulls. They used their strong jaws to strangle their opponents. Fortunately, these breeds can be gentle when raised in a loving environment.

The shar-pei's loose skin was originally developed to allow it to twist out of an opponent's jaws during a dog fight.

Above: *Young wolf puppies share many physical traits with dogs.*

Chapter 3

The Wolf Remains

Despite all the years of domestication and all the selective breeding for different behavioral and physical traits, the dog still retains the stamp of its wild wolf heritage. Even the tiniest poodle or chihuahua is still a wolf at heart.

THE PUPPY IN THE DOG

Some experts believe an important principle underlies much of our success in domesticating the wolf and developing it into the dog. Many of the traits we value in dogs are those more typical of young wolves than of adults. Compared to an adult wolf, a dog has a shorter face, a bigger head, larger eyes, and shorter legs; its tail curves upward, and its ears may flop over. All these are traits found in wolves before they are born. Some are lost even before birth, while others change as the wolf pup grows to adulthood.

Not only are the physical characteristics of dogs similar to those of young wolves, so are the behavioral traits. Like a

Opposite: *Even the samoyed, a huskylike northern breed, has a shorter muzzle than the wolf.*

young wolf, a properly socialized adult dog should look up to its elders (humans) for guidance, behaving submissively toward them. As wolves mature, however, they become more dominant in their behavior. They are also less likely to accept strangers. Adult wolves are more likely to fight with a strange wolf than accept it. Most adult dogs are at least tolerant of strangers and many are so friendly that they have to be restrained. Breeds like golden retrievers and some spaniels never seem to lose their innocent, charming puppy behavior. This is part of what makes them such wonderful family pets.

THE WOLF IN THE DOG

People who know both wolves and dogs are tempted to refer to dogs as "fractured wolves." But while domestication has changed the wolf in vital ways, many aspects of basic wolf behavior remain in its domesticated descendant. Just watch two strange dogs meet—you can see the dominance and submission at work very quickly. A confident dog is likely to approach a strange dog with its ears pricked forward and its

The dominant dog in front has a raised tail, while the other, more submissive dog's tail hangs down.

tail held high, just like a dominant wolf. A shy dog, on the other hand, may act submissively right from the start, lowering its tail, laying back its ears, and crouching. If the dominant dog continues its dominant behavior, the subordinate dog may roll over on its back, acting just like a submissive wolf.

Dogs behave toward humans in much the same ways as they do toward other dogs. Within a family, a dog treats people similarly to the way a wolf treats pack members. This can be good and bad. A properly trained dog learns that it is subordinate to the people in the family and will usually obey them. However, if people let a dog get the idea that it is the dominant leader, trouble results. Breeds such as golden retrievers and Australian shepherds tend easily to accept humans as dominant. But breeds like Siberian huskies and Scottish terriers are more likely to need firm discipline to keep them from taking over. When a dog becomes too dominant, it may growl at family members, refuse to obey commands, or even bite.

Left: *At least during this play session, Ninja—with raised tail—is dominant over Elsa, who like a subordinate wolf is lying low.*

Right: *In play, Ninja acts dominant with her human "pack mate" Jason, but she does so in a gentle manner, without using her teeth.*

Right: *Elsa acts submissively with Jason just like she does with Ninja—with tail tucked under, Elsa tries to get lower than Jason no matter how low Jason gets.*

Below: *Sometimes dogs scratch up the ground after urinating or defecating as a visual means of marking territory.*

When a dog encounters a person it considers dominant, it acts just as it would when meeting a dominant canine; it presses its ears back and wags its lowered tail. When the two get close together, and if the person continues to give strong, dominant signals, the dog is likely to roll over on its back submissively and may even urinate, behaving just like a submissive wolf.

A dominant dog, on the other hand, may approach a person with its ears pricked, tail raised, and perhaps its hackles raised. If you meet up with such a dog, don't run away. Running is likely to trigger the chase response in the dog, and you may be bitten. Instead, stay calm, keep your hands still, and let the dog come up and sniff at you. It's best not to stare directly at the strange dog, since staring is a form of challenge.

If you have a male dog, you have probably noticed that he is likely to stop at every tree, bush, and fire hydrant he sees, sniff at it intently, then lift his leg and urinate. Some female dogs also sniff at such signposts and urinate. This behavior is a message telling other dogs that come by that "I was here." Wolf packs use the same method to mark the boundaries of their territories. Each pack has its own area where it dens and hunts. If strange wolves enter this territory, they risk attack and death. Pack members periodically urinate on signposts around the borders of their territories to warn potential intruders to stay out.

One important difference between wolves and dogs is that wolves do not bark as often as dogs. But people find barking useful as a warning, and the tendency to bark was encouraged in breeding some dogs. Barking is natural to dogs and it can create real problems, especially when it is excessive, such as when a bored, confined dog keeps it up all day or all night.

Although barking is rare among wolves, howling is an important way wolves communicate with one another.

Puppies, whether they are wolf puppies chewing on bones or samoyeds playing with a tool box, chew on whatever they can find.

While barking has been encouraged in dogs, howling—one of the wolf's major means of communication—seems to have been suppressed. Wolves howl together before a hunt, and they howl when separated to keep in touch. Howling also keeps different packs aware of where neighboring packs live, so they can avoid one another. For these reasons, a wolf tends to howl in response to another wolf. But dogs rarely howl, except perhaps when they hear a siren. The siren seems to set off the ancient urge to respond to a faraway howl, and soon dogs all over the neighborhood are howling enthusiastically.

ASPECTS OF TAMING

Over thousands of years of developing the dog, people have selected against the more destructive individuals and have selected for those that could adapt their behavior to life with humans. But wolves are not as flexible. Even when raised by

Bud is performing the equivalent of a wolf's greeting by placing his paws on Barbara's shoulders and licking her chin.

people, most wolves become at least somewhat distant and wary as they grow up. Few captive wolves enjoy being petted by people. Even the tamest wolves treat their human "pack mates" much as they would other wolves, jumping up, placing paws on shoulders, and giving enthusiastic muzzle bites to a person's nose. While such a nip might not hurt a wolf, it can be painful for a person. Most dogs, on the other hand, seem to recognize humans as something different from other dogs. Even though they accept humans as their pack mates, well-adjusted dogs treat us differently and avoid using their teeth strongly in play as they do with other dogs. Wolves get into trouble through their more active exploration of their environment. They are much more thorough than dogs about chewing up toys and food bowls, shredding objects, and energetically digging up their pens.

Another important difference is in training. It is natural for dogs to want to please people who are their leaders, which can make training quite easy if their human companions understand how to communicate with them. But even captive wolves that have always lived with people may not share that concern. Pleasing people through obedient behavior just doesn't come naturally to a wolf. For this reason, people who live with tame wolves usually find that they must adapt their lives to the wolves', rather than the other way around.

Even though dogs like to please people, food rewards come in handy in obedience training.

OUR BEST FRIEND

The most important role of dogs today is to be our friends and companions. Dogs require loving attention, but they give back more than they receive. Dogs give their human companions unconditional love and are always there with an encouraging wag of the tail when they are needed. The dog is indeed a very special animal.

Chapter 4

Canines in Today's World

*I*n the twentieth century, humans have found new uses for dogs—jobs that take advantage of the love and loyalty of dogs and their willingness to work, rather than the special traits of any one breed.

VERY HELPFUL FRIENDS

Using dogs as helpers for the blind came first. A guide dog for the blind is trained to be its owner's eyes, watching for a variety of potential hazards, like cars on streets and overhanging branches above. A guide dog must be ever watchful, keeping the safety of its owner always in mind. Thousands of blind people live independent lives thanks to their guide dogs.

The guide dog idea has been expanded during recent years into other areas. Service dogs, for example, help people confined to wheelchairs by pulling the chairs, turning on light switches, pushing elevator buttons, and performing a variety

Glenn Martyn is training a hearing dog named Jasper to alert him to a knock at the door.

Opposite: Bo does a good job helping Diane Carrell.

39

Hugger and Suzie Foley take a break from their hard work of search and rescue training.

of other tasks. Hearing dogs serve as their owners' ears, alerting them to a baby's cry, ringing doorbells or telephones, whistling tea kettles, or cars behind them in the street.

Guide dogs and service dogs are usually specially bred for their jobs. They need to be large enough to assist the needs of their human companions and unafraid of new situations. They need to be able to get along amidst large groups of strangers and other dogs. Labrador and golden retrievers, and German shepherd dogs are popular breeds for this kind of work. Hearing dogs, however, perform a different type of work. Since a hearing dog signals an alert by jumping up and on a person, a dog that is not too big is best. Because they need less extensive training, hearing dogs are often chosen by trainers from young dogs left at animal shelters.

When people get lost, search and rescue dogs can often find them. With their very fine sense of smell, these dogs can follow a person's trail with ease, and they can even locate people in the rubble of fallen buildings after an earthquake.

Search and rescue dogs require their own special kind of training. Like guide and service dogs, they need to be unafraid of new and strange environments. They must also be especially athletic. They are trained to climb ladders and wriggle through small openings into dark places.

The dog's great sense of smell is also used to locate drugs in baggage at airports or to find bombs in packages. The dog is trained to respond to certain smells and to alert its handler when it senses them.

WOLVES IN OUR WORLD

Wolves once roamed the entire Northern Hemisphere. Now humans have populated much of the earth, and wolves survive in significant numbers in only a few areas. In Europe, wolves still live in the mountains of Greece and Spain. There are also wolves in the northern wildernesses of Russia and

There are still large numbers of wolves in Alaska.

China. In North America, many wolves live in wild parts of Alaska and Canada, but few inhabit the lower 48 states. Minnesota has more wolves than any other state besides Alaska, and a few also live in Wisconsin, Michigan, Idaho, Montana, and possibly Washington.

Many people are interested in returning wolves to the places they once lived. Wolves play an important role in keeping the balance of nature by preying on large animals. Without wolves, populations of animals like deer and elk could grow unchecked, resulting in overpopulation.

The two areas most promising for wolf reintroduction are Yellowstone National Park and the wild areas of New Mexico and Arizona. The wolf is the only large mammal **native** to Yellowstone that is now absent. Reintroducing wolves to

A Mexican wolf

Yellowstone would help reestablish the proper balance of nature in the park. A type of wolf called the Mexican wolf once lived in New Mexico and Arizona. There may be a few Mexican wolves still living in remote Mexican mountains, but none now survive in the United States, except in zoos and breeding centers. We can hope that sometime a good home in the wild will be found for Mexican wolves.

Animal shelters and humane societies are always looking for homes for animals like these puppies the author is holding.

DOGS IN OUR WORLD

Dogs have the opposite problem from wolves—there are too many of them. Every year, millions of dogs die because there are no homes for them. Altogether, in the United States today, there is about one dog for three people. Many of those dogs roam the streets of cities as strays, trying to find enough food in garbage cans and alleyways.

Too many people let their dogs breed, then turn the puppies over to animal shelters. Animal shelters try to adopt out homeless animals, but there are just not enough homes to go around.

The best way to control this overpopulation of dogs is to have pets spayed or neutered. Such surgery costs money, but it can save money and worry in the long run. A neutered male dog is much less likely to wander and become lost or get hit by a car than one that has not been neutered. Female dogs that have been spayed young have a much smaller chance of getting certain cancers than females that are not spayed early.

Puppies and children are a natural combination.

When you take the time to understand your canine companions, you'll find that dogs are adaptable and are willing to do anything—

—even jump rope.

CANINES AND PEOPLE

In any relationship, knowing what makes the other individual tick can help understanding. So when your dog behaves in ways that may seem strange, think of the wolf within. How might that fascinating ancestor be influencing your pet across the years of domestication? By looking at dogs as complex animals with needs and desires that reach back to their wild beginnings, we can appreciate their basic nature and understand them better. And by observing our canine companions, we can grasp something of what makes wolves such interesting and successful wild creatures that deserve their place in the natural order.

Just like children, every dog should be loved. We have developed this wonderful animal as our most loving and attentive companion. It is our responsibility to see that we keep our side of the bargain by loving, respecting, and caring well for our canine friends.

Further Reading

Wolves

Johnson, Sylvia J., and Aamodt, Alice. *Wolf Pack*. Minnesota: Lerner Publications Company, 1985.

Lawrence, R.D. *Wolves*. Massachusetts: Little, Brown & Company, 1990.

Mech, David L. *The Way of the Wolf*. Minnesota: Voyageur Press, 1991.

Patent, Dorothy Hinshaw. *Gray Wolf, Red Wolf*. New York: Clarion Books, 1990.

Dogs

American Kennel Club Staff, The. *The Complete Dog Book*. New York: Howell Book House, 1985.

Fox, Michael W. *Superdog: Raising the Perfect Canine Companion*. New York: Howell Book House, 1990.

Hart, Benjamen, and Hart, Lynnette, *The Perfect Puppy: How to Choose Your Dog by Its Behavior*. New York: W.H. Freeman & Company, 1987.

Monks of New Skete Staff, The. *How to be Your Dog's Best Friend*. Massachusetts: Little, Brown & Company, 1978.

Morris, Desmond. *Dogwatching*. New York: Crown Publishers, Inc., 1987.

Neil, David H., and Rutherford, Clarice. *How to Raise a Puppy You Can Live With*. Connecticut: Alpine Publications, 1982.

Anyone interested in wolves and dogs may want to join the International Wolf Center, Box 27, Ely, Minnesota, 55731, and receive a subscription to the quarterly magazine *International Wolf*.

Glossary

canine: having to do with dogs or the family Canidae

domesticate: to shape a species of animal over time to live with and assist humans

dominance hierarchy *(HI-er-ark-ee)*: the social structure of, for example, a wolf pack, which is based on a pecking order, in which each individual pack member has a rank

evolve: to go through a gradual process of change

instinct: an inborn response an animal has to its environment

native: originating and living naturally in a particular region

selective breeding: a method of changing or maintaining a kind of animal by the careful selection of parents who have the most desirable traits

submissive: behavior reflecting a lower rank

subordinate: occupying a lower rank or position

tame: to accustom an individual animal to the presence of humans

METRIC CONVERSION CHART		
WHEN YOU KNOW:	MULTIPLY BY:	TO FIND:
inches	2.54	centimeters
feet	.3048	meters
miles	1.609	kilometers
ounces	28.35	grams
pounds	.454	kilograms
gallons	3.787	liters

Index

Pages listed in **bold** type refer to photographs.